# THE HISTORY OF FOODS
# BREAKFAST FOODS

by Kristine Spanier, MLIS

pogo

# Ideas for Parents and Teachers

Pogo Books let children practice reading informational text while introducing them to nonfiction features such as headings, labels, sidebars, maps, and diagrams, as well as a table of contents, glossary, and index.

Carefully leveled text with a strong photo match offers early fluent readers the support they need to succeed.

## Before Reading

- "Walk" through the book and point out the various nonfiction features. Ask the student what purpose each feature serves.
- Look at the glossary together. Read and discuss the words.

## During Reading

- Have the child read the book independently.
- Invite them to list questions that arise from reading.

## After Reading

- Discuss the child's questions. Talk about how they might find answers to those questions.
- Prompt the child to think more. Ask: Were you surprised to learn people stole ideas when inventing breakfast foods? What more would you like to learn about the history of breakfast foods?

Pogo Books are published by Jump!
3500 American Blvd W, Suite 150
Bloomington, MN 55431
www.jumplibrary.com

Copyright © 2026 Jump!
International copyright reserved in all countries.
No part of this book may be reproduced in any form without written permission from the publisher.

Jump! is a division of FlutterBee Education Group.

Library of Congress Cataloging-in-Publication Data

Names: Spanier, Kristine, author.
Title: Breakfast foods / by Kristine Spanier, MLIS.
Description: Minneapolis, MN: Jump!, Inc., [2026]
Series: The history of foods | Includes index.
Audience: Ages 7-10
Identifiers: LCCN 2024053481 (print)
LCCN 2024053482 (ebook)
ISBN 9798892138970 (hardcover)
ISBN 9798892138987 (paperback)
ISBN 9798892138994 (ebook)
Subjects: LCSH: Breakfasts–History–Juvenile literature.
Inventors–History–Juvenile literature. | Inventions–History
–Juvenile literature.
Classification: LCC TX733 .S69 2026 (print)
LCC TX733 (ebook)
DDC 641.5/209–dc23/eng/20241228
LC record available at https://lccn.loc.gov/2024053481
LC ebook record available at https://lccn.loc.gov/2024053482

Editor: Jenna Gleisner
Designer: Molly Ballanger

Photo Credits: Pixel-Shot/Shutterstock, cover; Mega Pixel/Shutterstock, 1 (left); Sheila Fitzgerald/Shutterstock, 1 (right); digitalreflections/Shutterstock, 3 (left); Spalnic/Shutterstock, 3 (right); StockFedo/Shutterstock, 4 (left); powerofforever/Getty, 4 (right); Africa Studio/Shutterstock, 5; Picture Kitchen/Alamy, 6-7 (corn flakes); Sage Naumann/Shutterstock, 6-7 (kitten), 6-7 (coffee maker), 6-7 (school), 6-7 (house); Archive Photos/Getty, 6-7 (baseball), 12-13; Kazyavka/Shutterstock, 6-7 (background); Everett Collection, Old Visuals/Everett/SuperStock, 8; LauriPatterson/iStock, 9 (foreground); The Image Party/Shutterstock, 9 (background); IWei/Adobe Stock, 10-11; Steve Moss/Alamy, 14-15; Sheila Fitzgerald, 16-17; JeniFoto/Shutterstock, 17; My Childhood Memories/Alamy, 18; Noam Galai/Getty, 19; Shutterstock, 20 (Fruity Pebbles), 20 (Life), 20 (Mini-Wheats), 20 (Lucky Charms), 20 (Cinnamon Toast Crunch), 20 (Honey Bunches of Oats), 20 (Frosted Flakes), 20 (Cheerios); Walter Cicchetti/Adobe Stock, 20 (Froot Loops); Steve Cukrov/Adobe Stock, 20 (Honey Nut Cheerios); Image Source/iStock, 20-21; Keith Homan/Shutterstock, 23.

Printed in the United States of America at Corporate Graphics in North Mankato, Minnesota.

# TABLE OF CONTENTS

**CHAPTER 1**
A Lucky Mistake . . . . . . . . . . . . . . . . . . . . . . . . . . . . 4

**CHAPTER 2**
Fast Breakfast . . . . . . . . . . . . . . . . . . . . . . . . . . . . 8

**CHAPTER 3**
Selling Breakfast . . . . . . . . . . . . . . . . . . . . . . . . . 18

**QUICK FACTS & TOOLS**
Timeline . . . . . . . . . . . . . . . . . . . . . . . . . . . . . . . 22
Glossary . . . . . . . . . . . . . . . . . . . . . . . . . . . . . . . 23
Index . . . . . . . . . . . . . . . . . . . . . . . . . . . . . . . . . 24
To Learn More . . . . . . . . . . . . . . . . . . . . . . . . . 24

# CHAPTER 1

# A LUCKY MISTAKE

Did you know cereal was **invented** by mistake? In the late 1800s, Dr. John Kellogg wanted to make healthy food for people. He created a breakfast wheat bread.

Dr. John Kellogg

One night, the dough was left out. It dried and turned hard. John and his brother, Will, tried to fix it. They ran it through a **press**. It broke into flakes! They pressed dried corn dough, too. Dr. Kellogg's **patients** loved it! They ate it with milk. Corn flakes were invented!

CHAPTER 1

**1908 Corn Flakes advertisement**

CHAPTER 1

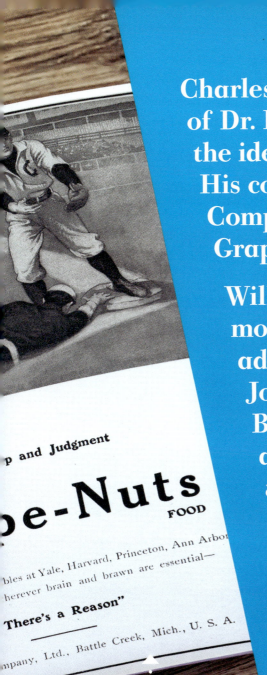

Charles William Post was one of Dr. Kellogg's patients. He stole the idea! He made his own cereal. His company was Postum Cereal Company. The cereal was called Grape-Nuts.

Will Kellogg wanted to sell more cereal. In 1906, he started adding sugar to the cereal. John did not like the idea. But they sold 100,000 boxes a day! Both companies **advertised** their **products**.

**DID YOU KNOW?**

When we sleep, we don't eat. This means we **fast**. In the morning, we break the fast when we eat. That is why it is called "breakfast!"

1909 Grape-Nuts advertisement

CHAPTER 1    7

# CHAPTER 2
# FAST BREAKFAST

In the 1930s, freezers became popular. Why? Frozen food does not rot. Three brothers started a food company. They were Frank, Tony, and Sam Dorsa. They tried freezing different foods.

freezer

The brothers made waffles. They froze and rewarmed them. They called them "froffles." People loved having waffles all the time. The brothers changed the name to Eggo. Why? It was their company name!

CHAPTER 2      9

CHAPTER 2

In the 1960s, Postum invented **pastries**. They were called Country Squares. They could be heated in a toaster. But Postum wasn't ready to sell them. The Kellogg Company heard about the idea. It made its own **version** first. It called them Pop-Tarts.

## WHAT DO YOU THINK?

Pop-Tarts originally had four **flavors**. They were strawberry, blueberry, apple currant, and brown sugar cinnamon. Now, there are almost 100 flavors! What flavor would you invent?

CHAPTER 2   11

Quaker has been selling oatmeal since 1850. In 1966, it created instant oatmeal. You just add hot water! Families loved it. In 1970, the first flavor was made. It was maple and brown sugar.

### WHAT DO YOU THINK?

Cereals loaded with sugar were popular in the 1970s. Some new **brands** were Lucky Charms, Apple Jacks, and Frosted Mini Wheats. Do you think cereal should have more or less sugar? Why?

CHAPTER 2

McDonald's made the Egg McMuffin in 1971. It was the first fast-food breakfast sandwich. Soon, other restaurants made them, too.

CHAPTER 2

CHAPTER 2

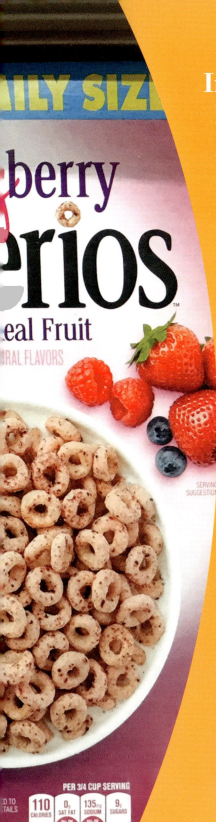

In the 1990s, people wanted healthier breakfasts. Companies **marketed** "whole grain" and "low sugar" on cereal boxes. Granola and Greek yogurt became popular. Americans were returning to the ideas of Dr. Kellogg!

granola

yogurt

CHAPTER 2   17

# CHAPTER 3
# SELLING BREAKFAST

Since cereal was invented, companies have worked hard to sell their product. They put free items inside the boxes. Postum included small books. Kellogg's added **coupons** for kids' books. Plastic toys became popular, too.

Today, cereal boxes have bright colors. They stand out. Many have fun games and puzzles on the back! There are fun cereal ads, too. Famous characters include Tony the Tiger and the Trix Rabbit. Ads have **slogans** like, "L'eggo my Eggo!" They help us remember product names.

CHAPTER 3 19

# TAKE A LOOK!

What are the top 10 most sold cereals? How many boxes are sold each year? Take a look!

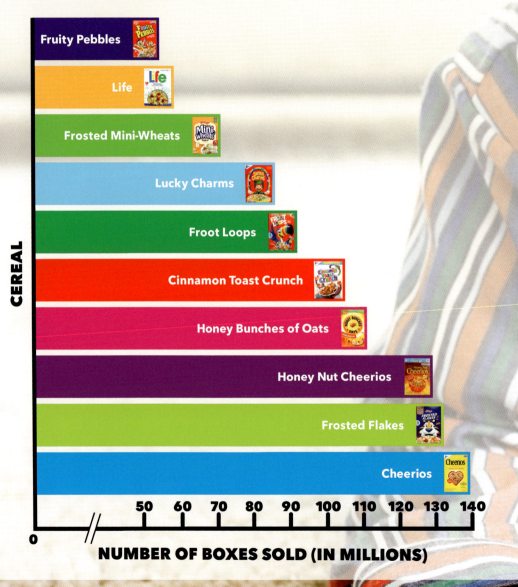

Breakfast is a fun part of our day. We have many choices. What is your favorite breakfast food?

CHAPTER 3

# QUICK FACTS & TOOLS

## TIMELINE

**Take a look at some important dates in the history of breakfast foods!**

**1894**
Dr. John Kellogg and his brother, Will, make the first cereal flakes.

**1895**
Charles William Post starts the Postum Cereal Company.

**1953**
The Dorsa brothers invent frozen waffles.

**1964**
Kellogg's introduces Pop-Tarts.

**1966**
Quaker invents instant oatmeal.

**1971**
McDonald's invents the Egg McMuffin.

**1990s**
Granola and Greek yogurt become popular breakfast foods.

**2020s**
Cheerios is the best-selling cereal on the market.

# GLOSSARY

**advertised:** Showed or told about a product or service using commercials, posters, or other methods so people want to buy or use it.

**brands:** Names that identify a product or the company that makes it.

**coupons:** Small pieces of paper that give a discount on something.

**fast:** To go without eating for a period of time.

**flavors:** Tastes.

**invented:** Created and produced for the first time.

**marketed:** Shared information about a product to convince people to buy it.

**pastries:** Pies, tarts, or other sweet baked goods.

**patients:** People who receive medical care and treatment.

**press:** A machine that uses pressure to shape, flatten, squeeze, or stamp.

**products:** Items that are made, grown, or created to be sold or used by people.

**slogans:** Words or phrases used to attract attention.

**version:** A different or changed form of something.

QUICK FACTS & TOOLS 23

# INDEX

advertised 7
brands 12
cereal 4, 7, 12, 17, 18, 19, 20
corn flakes 5
Country Squares 11
Dorsa brothers 8, 9
Egg McMuffin 14
Eggo 9, 19
flavors 11, 12
frozen food 8, 9
granola 17
Grape-Nuts 7

Greek yogurt 17
Kellogg Company 11, 18
Kellogg, John 4, 5, 7, 17
Kellogg, Will 5, 7
marketed 17
McDonald's 14
Pop-Tarts 11
Post, Charles William 7
Postum Cereal Company 7, 11, 18
products 7, 18, 19
Quaker instant oatmeal 12
slogans 19

# TO LEARN MORE

Finding more information is as easy as 1, 2, 3.
1. Go to www.factsurfer.com
2. Enter "breakfastfoods" into the search box.
3. Choose your book to see a list of websites.

QUICK FACTS & TOOLS